Your Native Land,
Your Life

ADRIENNE RICH

Your Native Land, Your Life

POEMS

W·W·NORTON & COMPANY

New York · London

Some of these poems first appeared in the following periodicals: *The Boston Review,*
I-KON, Parnassus, Peace and Freedom, River Styx, San José Studies, and *Sojourner.* "Sources"
was first published as a chapbook by The Heyeck Press, Woodside, California.
"Upcountry" and "Poetry: III" were first published as broadsides by The Heyeck Press.

Printed in the United States of America

The text of this book is composed in Garamond, with
display type set in Centaur. Composition and
manufacturing by Maple-Vail Book Manufacturing Group.
Book design by Antonina Krass.

Library of Congress Cataloging-in-Publication Data
Rich, Adrienne.
Your native land, your life.
I. Title
PS3535.I233Y6   1986   811'.54   85-28525

ISBN 0-393-31082-5

W. W. Norton & Company, Inc., 500 Fifth Avenue, New York, NY 10110
W. W. Norton & Company Ltd, 10 Coptic Street, London WC1A 1PU
1   2   3   4   5   6   7   8   9   0

Contents

vii

I

Sources

For Helen Smelser
—since 1949—

I

Sixteen years.   The narrow, rough-gullied backroads
almost the same.   The farms: almost the same,
a new barn here, a new roof there, a rusting car,
collapsed sugar-house, trailer, new young wife
trying to make a lawn instead of a dooryard,
new names, old kinds of names: Rocquette, Desmarais,
Clark, Pierce, Stone.   Gossier.   No names of mine.

The vixen I met at twilight on Route 5
south of Willoughby: long dead.   She was an omen
to me, surviving, herding her cubs
in the silvery bend of the road
in nineteen sixty-five.

Shapes of things: so much the same
they feel like eternal forms: the house and barn
on the rise above May Pond; the brow of Pisgah;
the face of milkweed blooming,
brookwater pleating over slanted granite,
boletus under pine, the half-composted needles
it broke through patterned on its skin.
Shape of queen anne's lace, with the drop of blood.
Bladder-campion veined with purple.
Multifoliate heal-all.

II

I refuse to become a seeker for cures.
Everything that has ever
helped me has come through what already
lay stored in me.   Old things, diffuse, unnamed, lie strong
across my heart.
                    This is from where
my strength comes, even when I miss my strength
even when it turns on me
like a violent master.

III

From where?   the voice asks coldly.

This is the voice in cold morning air
that pierces dreams.   *From where does your strength come?*

Old things . . .
                    From where does your strength come, you Southern Jew?
split at the root, raised in a castle of air?

Yes.   I expected this.   I have known for years
the question was coming.   *From where*

(not from these, surely,
Protestant separatists, Jew-baiters, nightriders

who fired in Irasburg in nineteen-sixty-eight
on a black family newly settled in these hills)
                                        From where

the dew grows thick late August on the fierce green grass
and on the wooden sill and on the stone

the mountains stand in an extraordinary
point of no return   though still are green

collapsed shed-boards gleam like pewter in the dew
the realms of touch-me-not   fiery with tiny tongues

cover the wild ground of the woods

IV

With whom do you believe your lot is cast?
From where does your strength come?

I think somehow, somewhere
every poem of mine must repeat those questions

which are not the same.   There is a *whom,* a *where*
that is not chosen   that is given   and sometimes falsely given

in the beginning we grasp whatever we can
to survive

V

All during World War II
I told myself I had some special destiny:
there had to be a reason
I was not living in a bombed-out house
or cellar   hiding out with rats

there had to be a reason
I was growing up safe, American
with sugar rationed in a Mason jar

split at the root   white-skinned social christian
neither gentile nor Jew

through the immense silence
of the Holocaust

I had no idea of what I had been spared

still less of the women and men   my kin
the Jews of Vicksburg or Birmingham
whose lives must have been strategies no less
than the vixen's on Route 5

VI

If they had played the flute, or chess
I was told   I was not told what they told
their children when the Klan rode
how they might have seen themselves

a chosen people

of shopkeepers
clinging by strategy to a way of life
that had its own uses for them

proud of their length of sojourn in America
deploring the late-comers   the peasants from Russia

I saw my father building
his rootless ideology

his private castle in air

in that most dangerous place, the family home
we were the chosen people

In the beginning we grasp whatever we can

VII

For years I struggled with you: your categories, your theories, your will, the cruelty which came inextricable from your love.   For years all arguments I carried on in my head were with you.   I saw myself, the eldest daughter raised as a son, taught to study but not to pray, taught to hold reading and writing sacred: the eldest daughter in a house with no son, she who must overthrow the father, take what he taught her and use it against him.   All this in a castle of air, the floating world of the assimilated who know and deny they will always be aliens.

After your death I met you again as the face of patriarchy, could name at last precisely the principle you embodied, there was an ideology at last which let me dispose of you, identify the suffering you caused, hate you righteously as part of a system, the kingdom of the fathers.   I saw the power and arrogance of the male as your true watermark; I did not see beneath it the suffering of the Jew, the alien stamp you bore, because you had deliberately arranged that it should be invisible to me.   It is only now, under a powerful, womanly lens, that I can decipher your suffering and deny no part of my own.

VIII

Back there in Maryland the stars
showed liquescent, diffuse

in the breathless summer nights
the constellations melted

I thought I was leaving a place of enervation
heading north where the Drinking Gourd

stood cold and steady at last
pointing the way

I thought I was following a track of freedom
and for awhile it was

IX

Why has my imagination stayed
northeast with the ones who stayed

Are there spirits in me, diaspora-driven
that wanted to lodge somewhere

hooked into the "New" Englanders who hung on
here in this stringent space

believing their Biblical language
their harping on righteousness?

And, myself apart, what was this like for them,
this unlikely growing season

after each winter so mean, so mean
the tying-down of the spirit

and the endless rocks in the soil, the endless
purifications of self

there being no distance, no space around
to experiment with life?

X

These upland farms are the farms
of invaders, these villages

white with rectitude and death
are built on stolen ground

The persecuted, pale with anger
know how to persecute

those who feel destined, under god's eye
need never ponder difference

and if they kill others for being who they are
or where they are

is this a law of history
or simply, *what must change?*

XI

If I try to conjure their lives
—who are not my people by any definition—

Yankee Puritans, Québec Catholics
mingled within sight of the Northern Lights

I am forced to conjure a passion
like the tropism in certain plants

bred of a natural region's
repetitive events

beyond the numb of poverty
christian hypocrisy, isolation

—a passion so unexpected
there is no name for it

so quick, fierce, unconditional
short growing season is no explanation.

XII

And has any of this to do with how
Mohawk or Wampanoag knew it?

is the passion I connect with in this air
trace of the original

existences that knew this place
is the region still trying to speak with them

is this light a language
the shudder of this aspen-grove a way

of sending messages
the white mind barely intercepts

are signals also coming back
from the vast diaspora

of the people who kept their promises
as a way of life?

XIII

Coming back after sixteen years
I stare anew at things

that steeple pure and righteous
that clapboard farmhouse

seeing what I hadn't seen before
through barnboards, crumbling plaster

decades of old wallpaper roses
clinging to certain studs

—into that dangerous place
the family home:

There are verbal brutalities
borne thereafter like any burn or scar

there are words pulled down from the walls
like dogwhips

the child backed silent against the wall
trying to keep her eyes dry;   haughty;   in panic

I will never let you know
I will never
let you know

XIV

And if my look becomes the bomb that rips
the family home apart

is this betrayal, that the walls
slice off, the staircase shows

torn-away above the street
that the closets where the clothes hung

hang naked, the room the old
grandmother had to sleep in

the toilet on the landing
the room with the books

where the father walks up and down
telling the child to *work, work*

harder than anyone has worked before?
—But I can't stop seeing like this

more and more I see like this everywhere.

XV

It's an oldfashioned, an outrageous thing
to believe one has a "destiny"

—a thought often peculiar to those
who possess privilege—

but there is something else: the faith
of those despised and endangered

that they are not merely the sum
of damages done to them:

have kept beyond violence the knowledge
arranged in patterns like kente-cloth

unexpected as in batik
recurrent as bitter herbs and unleavened bread

of being a connective link
in a long, continuous way

of ordering hunger, weather, death, desire
and the nearness of chaos.

XVI

The Jews I've felt rooted among
are those who were turned to smoke

Reading of the chimneys against the blear air
I think I have seen them myself

the fog of northern Europe licking its way
along the railroad tracks

to the place where all tracks end
You told me not to look there

to become
a citizen of the world

bound by no tribe or clan
yet dying you followed the Six Day War

with desperate attention
and this summer I lie awake at dawn

sweating the Middle East through my brain
wearing the star of David

on a thin chain at my breastbone

XVII

But there was also the other Jew. The one you most feared, the one from the *shtetl*, from Brooklyn, from the wrong part of history, the wrong accent, the wrong class. The one I left you for.   The one both like and unlike you, who explained you to me for years, who could not explain himself.   The one who said, as if he had memorized the formula, *There's nothing left now but the food and the humor*.   The one who, like you, ended isolate, who had tried to move in the floating world of the assimilated who know and deny they will always be aliens.   Who drove to Vermont in a rented car at dawn and shot himself.   For so many years I had thought you and he were in opposition. I needed your unlikeness then; now it's your likeness that stares me in the face.   There is something more than food, humor, a turn of phrase, a gesture of the hands: there is something more.

XVIII

There is something more than self-hatred. That still outlives
these photos of the old Ashkenazi life:
we are gifted children at camp in the country
or orphaned children in kindergarten
we are hurrying along the rare book dealers' street
with the sunlight striking one side
we are walking the wards of the Jewish hospital
along diagonal squares   young serious nurses
we are part of a family group
formally taken in 1936
with tables,armchairs, ferns
(behind us, in our lives, the muddy street
and the ragged shames
the street-musician, the weavers lined for strike)
we are part of a family wearing white head-bandages
we were beaten in a pogrom

The place where all tracks end
is the place where history was meant to stop
but does not stop   where thinking
was meant to stop but does not stop
where the pattern was meant to give way at last
                                        but only
becomes a different pattern
                            terrible, threadbare
strained   familiar   on-going

XIX

They say such things are stored
in the genetic code—

half-chances, unresolved
possibilities, the life

passed on because unlived—
a mystic biology?—

I think of the women who sailed to Palestine
years before I was born—

halutzot, pioneers
believing in a new life

socialists, anarchists, jeered
as excitable, sharp of tongue

too filled with life
wanting equality in the promised land

carrying the broken promises
of Zionism in their hearts

along with the broken promises
of communism, anarchism—

makers of miracle who expected miracles
as stubbornly as any housewife does

that the life she gives her life to
shall not be cheap

that the life she gives her life to
shall not turn on her

that the life she gives her life to
shall want an end to suffering

Zion by itself is not enough.

XX

The faithful drudging child
the child at the oak desk whose penmanship,
hard work, style will win her prizes
becomes the woman with a mission, not to win prizes
but to change the laws of history.
How she gets this mission
is not clear, how the boundaries of perfection
explode, leaving her cheekbone grey with smoke
a piece of her hair singed off, her shirt
spattered with earth . . . Say that she grew up in a house
with talk of books, ideal societies—
she is gripped by a blue, a foreign air,
a desert absolute: dragged by the roots of her own will
into another scene of choices.

XXI

YERUSHALAYIM: a vault of golden heat
hard-pulsing from bare stones

the desert's hard-won, delicate green
the diaspora of the stars

thrilling like thousand-year-old locusts
audible yet unheard

a city on a hill
waking with first light to voices

piercing, original, intimate
as if my dreams mixed with the cries

of the oldest, earliest birds
and of all whose wrongs and rights

cry out for explication
as the night pales and one more day

breaks on this *Zion* of hope and fear
and broken promises
                              this promised land

XXII

I have resisted this for years, writing to you as if you could hear me. It's been different with my father: he and I always had a kind of rhetoric going with each other, a battle between us, it didn't matter if one of us was alive or dead. But, you, I've had a sense of protecting your existence, not using it merely as a theme for poetry or tragic musings; letting you dwell in the minds of those who have reason to miss you, in your way, or their way, not mine. The living, writers especially, are terrible projectionists. I hate the way they use the dead.

Yet I can't finish this without speaking to you, not simply of you. You knew there was more left than food and humor. Even as you said that in 1953 I knew it was a formula you had found, to stand between you and pain. The deep crevices of black pumpernickel under the knife, the sweet butter and red onions we ate on those slices; the lox and cream cheese on fresh onion rolls; bowls of sour cream mixed with cut radishes, cucumber, scallions; green tomatoes and kosher dill pickles in half-translucent paper; these, you said, were the remnants of the culture, along with the fresh *challah* which turned stale so fast but looked so beautiful.

That's why I want to speak to you now. To say: no person, trying to take responsibility for her or his identity, should have to be so alone. There must be those among whom we can sit down and weep, and still be counted as warriors. (I make up this strange, angry packet for you, threaded with love.) I think you thought there was no such place for you, and perhaps there was none then, and perhaps there is none now; but we will have to make it, we who want an end to suffering, who want to change the laws of history, if we are not to *give ourselves away*.

XXIII

Sixteen years ago I sat in this northeast kingdom
reading Gilbert White's *Natural History
of Selborne*   thinking
I can never know this land I walk upon
as that English priest knew his
—a comparable piece of earth—
rockledge   soil   insect   bird   weed   tree

I will never know it so well because . . .

*Because you have chosen
something else: to know other things
even the cities which
create of this a myth*

*Because you grew up in a castle of air
disjunctured*

*Because without a faith
                    you are faithful*

I have wished I could rest among the beautiful and common weeds
I cán name, both here and in other tracts of the globe.   But there
is no finite knowing, no such rest.   Innocent birds, deserts, morn-
ing-glories, point to choices. leading away from the familiar. When
I speak of an end to suffering I don't mean anesthesia. I mean know-
ing the world, and my place in it, not in order to stare with bitter-
ness or detachment, but as a powerful and womanly series of
choices: and here I write the words, in their fullness:
powerful;   womanly.

August 1981–
August 1982

II

North American
Time

For the Record

The clouds and the stars didn't wage this war
the brooks gave no information
if the mountain spewed stones of fire into the river
it was not taking sides
the raindrop faintly swaying under the leaf
had no political opinions

and if here or there a house
filled with backed-up raw sewage
or poisoned those who lived there
with slow fumes, over years
the houses were not at war
nor did the tinned-up buildings

intend to refuse shelter
to homeless old women and roaming children
they had no policy to keep them roaming
or dying, no, the cities were not the problem
the bridges were non-partisan
the freeways burned, but not with hatred

Even the miles of barbed-wire
stretched around crouching temporary huts
designed to keep the unwanted
at a safe distance, out of sight
even the boards that had to absorb
year upon year, so many human sounds

so many depths of vomit, tears
slow-soaking blood
had not offered themselves for this
The trees didn't volunteer to be cut into boards

nor the thorns for tearing flesh
Look around at all of it

and ask whose signature
is stamped on the orders, traced
in the corner of the building plans
Ask where the illiterate, big-bellied
women were, the drunks and crazies,
the ones you fear most of all: ask where you were.

1983

North American Time

I
When my dreams showed signs
of becoming
politically correct
no unruly images
escaping beyond borders
when walking in the street I found my
themes cut out for me
knew what I would not report
for fear of enemies' usage
then I began to wonder

II
Everything we write
will be used against us
or against those we love.
These are the terms,
take them or leave them.
Poetry never stood a chance
of standing outside history.
One line typed twenty years ago
can be blazed on a wall in spraypaint
to glorify art as detachment
or torture of those we
did not love but also
did not want to kill

We move   but our words stand
become responsible
for more than we intended

and this is verbal privilege

III
Try sitting at a typewriter
one calm summer evening
at a table by a window
in the country, try pretending
your time does not exist
that you are simply you
that the imagination simply strays
like a great moth, unintentional
try telling yourself
you are not accountable
to the life of your tribe
the breath of your planet

IV
It doesn't matter what you think.
Words are found responsible
all you can do is choose them
or choose
to remain silent.   Or, you never had a choice,
which is why the words that do stand
are responsible

and this is verbal privilege

V
Suppose you want to write
of a woman braiding
another woman's hair—
straight down, or with beads and shells
in three-strand plaits or corn-rows—
you had better know the thickness
the length   the pattern
why she decides to braid her hair
how it is done to her

what country it happens in
what else happens in that country

You have to know these things

VI
Poet, sister: words—
whether we like it or not—
stand in a time of their own.
No use protesting   *I wrote that*
before Kollontai was exiled
Rosa Luxemburg, Malcolm,
Anna Mae Aquash, murdered,
before Treblinka, Birkenau,
Hiroshima, before Sharpeville,
Biafra, Bangladesh, Boston,
Atlanta, Soweto, Beirut, Assam
—those faces, names of places
sheared from the almanac
of North American time

VII
I am thinking this in a country
where words are stolen out of mouths
as bread is stolen out of mouths
where poets don't go to jail
for being poets, but for being
dark-skinned, female, poor.
I am writing this in a time
when anything we write
can be used against those we love
where the context is never given
though we try to explain, over and over
For the sake of poetry at least
I need to know these things

VIII

Sometimes, gliding at night
in a plane over New York City
I have felt like some messenger
called to enter, called to engage
this field of light and darkness.
A grandiose idea, born of flying.
But underneath the grandiose idea
is the thought that what I must engage
after the plane has raged onto the tarmac
after climbing my old stairs, sitting down
at my old window
is meant to break my heart and reduce me to silence.

IX

In North America time stumbles on
without moving, only releasing
a certain North American pain.
Julia de Burgos wrote:
That my grandfather was a slave
is my grief;   had he been a master
that would have been my shame.
A poet's words, hung over a door
in North America, in the year
nineteen-eighty-three.
The almost-full moon rises
timelessly speaking of change
out of the Bronx, the Harlem River
the drowned towns of the Quabbin
the pilfered burial mounds
the toxic swamps, the testing-grounds

and I start to speak again

1983

Education of a Novelist

(Italicized lines quoted from Ellen Glasgow's
autobiography, *The Woman Within*.)

I

Looking back   trying to decipher
yourself and Lizzie Jones:

                         We were strange companions, but
that everyone knew us: a dark
lean, eager colored woman
and a small, pale, eager little girl
roaming together, hand-in-hand

Waking early, Mammy and I
would be dressed before the family had risen
spurred on by an inborn love
                         of adventure
a vital curiosity
               . . . visiting
the neighbors and the neighbors' cooks and *with the neighbors' maids*
   sweeping the brick pavement
                       and the apothecary
and the friendly light-colored letter-carrier

But when you made one visit to the almshouse
"Mammy" was reprimanded

II

I revolted from sentimentality
less because it was false then because
it was cruel . . .
               In the country, later
the Black artist spent her genius on the white children
Mammy was with us; we were all happy together

(I revolted from sentimentality   when it suited me)

She would dress us as gypsies, darken
our faces with burnt cork

                        We would start
on a long journey, telling fortunes
wherever we came to a farm or a Negro cabin
I was always the one who would
think up the most exciting fortunes

                                (I, too, was always the one)

III
Where or how I learned to read
(you boast so proudly)   *I could never*
remember   After supper
in front of the fire, undressing by candlelight
Mammy and I would take up and spin out
the story left from the evening before

Nobody ever taught me to read
                                (Nobody had to,
it was your birthright, Ellen.)

"As soon as I learn my letters,
Mammy, I'm going to teach you yours"

IV
Givens, Ellen. That we'd *pick out our way*
through the Waverly novels
that our childish, superior fire
was destined for fortune
even though female   deaf   or lame

3 8

dewomanized   The growing suspicion
haunting the growing life

the sense of exile in a hostile world
how do we use that?

                    and for what?

                              with whom?

Givens.   The pale skin, the eager look, the fact
of having been known
                    by everyone
our childish, superior fire, and all
I was always the one . . .
                    Deafness finally drives you
here, there, to specialists in Europe
for hardening of the Eustachian tube

Finding no cure you build
a wall of deceptive gaiety   to shield your pain:
That I, who was winged for flying, should be
wounded and caged!

V
Lizzie Jones vanishes.   Her trace is lost.
She, who was winged for flying

                    Where at the end
of the nineteenth century   you ask
could one find the Revolution?
In what mean streets and alleys of the South
was it then lying in ambush?   Though I suffered
with the world's suffering. . . .

> *"As soon*
as I learn my letters, Mammy,
I'm going to teach you yours"
> but by your own admission
you never did

Where at the end of the twentieth century
does the Revolution find us
in what streets and alleys, north or south
is it now lying in ambush?

> It's not enough
using your words to damn you, Ellen:
they could have been my own:
> this criss-cross
map of kept and broken promises
> *I was always the one*

1983

Virginia 1906

A white woman dreaming of innocence,
of a country childhood, apple-blossom driftings,
is held in a DC-10 above the purity
of a thick cloud ceiling in a vault of purest blue.
She feels safe.   Here, no one can reach her.
Neither men nor women have her in their power.

Because I have sometimes been her, because I am of her,
I watch her with eyes that blink away like a flash
cruelly, when she does what I don't want to see.
I am tired of innocence and its uselessness,
sometimes the dream of innocence beguiles me.
Nothing has told me how to think of her power.

Blurredly, apple-blossom drifts
across rough earth, small trees contort and twist
making their own shapes, wild.   Why should we love purity?
Can the woman in the DC-10 see this
and would she call this innocence?   If no one can reach her
she is drawing on unnamed, unaccountable power.

This woman I have been and recognize
must know that beneath the quilt of whiteness lies
a hated nation, hers,
earth whose wet places call to mind
still-open wounds: her country.
Do we love purity?   Where do we turn for power?

Knowing us as I do I cringe when she says
But I was not culpable,
I was the victim, the girl, the youngest,
the susceptible one, I was sick,

the one who simply had to get out, and did
: I am still trying how to think of her power.

And if she was forced, this woman, by the same
white Dixie boy who took for granted as prey
her ignored dark sisters?   What if at five years old
she was old to his fingers splaying her vulva open
what if forever after, in every record
she wants her name inscribed as *innocent*

and will not speak, refuses to know, can say
I have been numb for years
does not want to hear of any violation
like or unlike her own, as if the victim
can be innocent only in isolation
as if the victim dare not be intelligent

(I have been numb for years):   and if this woman
longs for an intact world, an intact soul,
longs for what we all long for, yet denies us all?
What has she smelled of power without once
tasting it in the mouth? For what protections
has she traded her wildness and the lives of others?

There is a porch in Salem, Virginia
that I have never seen, that may no longer stand,
honeysuckle vines twisting above the talk,
a driveway full of wheeltracks, paths going down
to the orchards, apple and peach,
divisions so deep a wild child lost her way.

A child climbing an apple-tree in Virginia
refuses to come down, at last comes down
for a neighbor's lying bribe.   Now, if that child, grown old
feels safe in a DC-10 above thick white clouds

and no one can reach her
and if that woman's child, another woman

chooses another way, yet finds the old vines
twisting across her path, the old wheeltracks
how does she stop dreaming the dream
of protection, how does she follow her own wildness
shedding the innocence, the childish power?
How does she keep from dreaming the old dreams?

1983

Dreams Before Waking

Despair is the question.
—Elie Wiesel

Hasta tu país cambió. Lo has cambiado tú mismo.
—Nancy Morejón

Despair falls:
the shadow of a building
they are raising in the direct path
of your slender ray of sunlight
Slowly the steel girders grow
the skeletal framework rises
yet the western light still filters
through it all
still glances off the plastic sheeting
they wrap around it
for dead of winter

At the end of winter something changes
a faint subtraction
from consolations you expected
an innocent brilliance that does not come
though the flower shops set out
once again on the pavement
their pots of tight-budded sprays
the bunches of jonquils stiff with cold
and at such a price
though someone must buy them
you study those hues as if with hunger

Despair falls
like the day you come home
from work, a summer evening
transparent with rose-blue light

and see they are filling in
the framework
the girders are rising
beyond your window
that seriously you live
in a different place
though you have never moved

and will not move, not yet
but will give away
your potted plants to a friend
on the other side of town
along with the cut crystal flashing
in the window-frame
will forget the evenings
of watching the street, the sky
the planes in the feathered afterglow:
will learn to feel grateful simply for this foothold

where still you can manage
to go on paying rent
where still you can believe
it's the old neighborhood:
even the woman who sleeps at night
in the barred doorway—wasn't she always there?
and the man glancing, darting
for food in the supermarket trash—
when did his hunger come to this?
what made the difference?
what will make it for you?

What will make it for you?
You don't want to know the stages
and those who go through them don't want to tell
You have your four locks on the door

your savings, your respectable past
your strangely querulous body, suffering
sicknesses of the city no one can name
You have your pride, your bitterness
your memories of sunset
you think you can make it straight through
if you don't speak of despair.

What would it mean to live
in a city whose people were changing
each other's despair into hope?—
You yourself must change it.—
what would it feel like to know
your country was changing?—
You yourself must change it.—
Though your life felt arduous
new and unmapped and strange
what would it mean to stand on the first
page of the end of despair?

1983

When / Then

Tell us
>>> *how we'll be together*
>>>>>> *in that time*

patch of sun on a gritty floor; an old newspaper, torn
for toilet paper and coughed-up scum   Don't talk, she said

when we still love but are no longer young

they bring you a raw purple stick and say
it is one of her fingers;   it could be
>>>>>> *Tell us*
about aging, what it costs, how women
have loved forty, fifty years
>>>>> enamel basin, scraped
down to the bare iron   some ashen hairs   red fluid
they say is her blood   how can you

Tell us about the gardens we will keep, the milk
we'll drink from our own goats
>>>>> she needs
anti-biotics they say which will be given
when you name names   they show you her fever chart

Tell us about community   *the joy*
of coming to rest

>>> *among women*
>>>>> *who will love us*

you choose between your community
and her   later others

will come through the cell   not all of them will love you
whichever way you choose

Don't talk, she said   (you will learn to hear
only her voice when they close in on you)   Don't talk

Why are you telling us this?

                              patch of sun on a gritty
floor, bad dreams, a torn newspaper, someone's blood
in a scraped basin. . . .

1983

Upcountry

The silver shadow   where the line falls grey
and pearly   the unborn villages quivering
under the rock   the snail   travelling the crevice
the furred, flying white insect like a tiny
intelligence lacing the air
this woman whose lips lie parted
after long speech
her white hair unrestrained

All that you never paid
or have with difficulty paid
attention to

Change and be forgiven!   the roots of the forest
muttered   but you tramped through   guilty
unable to take forgiveness   neither do you
give mercy

She is asleep now   dangerous   her mind
slits the air like silk   travels faster than sound
like scissors flung into the next century

Even as you watch for the trout's hooked stagger
across the lake   the crack of light and the crumpling bear
her mind was on them first
                         when forgiveness ends
her love means danger

1983

49

One Kind of Terror: A Love Poem

1.

From 1964: a color snapshot: you
riding a camel past the Great Pyramid

its rough earthy diagonal shouldering
the blue triangle of sky

I know your white shirt   dark skirt   your age
thirty-five   as mine was then

your ignorance like mine
in those years   and your curious mind

throw of your head   bend of your gilt knees
the laugh exchanged with whoever took the picture

I don't know how you were talking to yourself
I know I was thinking

with a schoolgirl's ardent rectitude
this will be the deciding year

I am sick of drift
Weren't we always trying to do better?

Then the voices began to say: *Your plans*
are not in the book of plans

written, printed and bound while you
were absent
                    no, not here nor in Egypt
will you ever catch up

2.
So, then   as if by plan
I turn   and you are lost

How have I lived   knowing
that day of your laugh   so alive/so nothing

even the clothes you wore then
rotted away   How can I live believing

any year can be the deciding year
when I know the book of plans

how it disallows us
time for change   for growing older

truthfully   in our own way

3.
I used to think you ought to be
a woman   in charge   in a desperate time

of whole populations
such seemed the power of your restlessness

I saw you a rescuer
amid huge events   diasporas

scatterings and returnings
I needed this for us

I would have gone to help you
flinging myself into the fray

both of us treading free

of the roads we started on

4.
In the book of plans it is written
that our lifelines shall be episodic

faithless   frayed   lived out
under impure violent rains

and rare but violent sun
It is written there that we may reach

like wan vines across a window
trying to grasp each other

but shall lack care and tending
that water and air shall betray us

that the daughter born a poet
will die of dysentery

while the daughter born to organize
will die of cancer

5.
In the book of plans it says no one
will speak of the book of plans

the appearance will continue
that all this is natural

It says my grief for you is natural
but my anger for us is not

that the image of a white curtain trembling

across a stormy pane

is acceptable   but not
the image I make of you

arm raised hurling   signalling
the squatters   the refugees

storming the food supply
The book of plans says only that you must die

that we all, very soon, must die

6.
Well, I am studying a different book
taking notes wherever I go

the movement of the wrist does not change
but the pen plows deeper

my handwriting flows into words
I have not yet spoken

I'm the sole author of nothing
the book moves from field to field

of testimony   recording
how the wounded teach each other   the old

refuse to be organized
by fools   how the women say

in more than one language   *You have struck a rock—*
prepare to meet the unplanned

the ignored   the unforeseen   that which breaks
despair   which has always travelled

underground   or in the spaces
between the fixed stars

gazing full-faced   wild
and calm   on the Revolution

7.
Love: I am studying a different book
and yes, a book is a finite thing

In it your death will never be reversed
the deaths I have witnessed since   never undone

The light drained from the living eyes
can never flash again from those same eyes

I make you no promises
but something's breaking open here

there were certain extremes we had to know
before we could continue

Call it a book, or not
call it a map of constant travel

Call it a book, or not
call it a song   a ray

of images thrown on a screen
in open lots   in cellars

and among those images
one woman's meaning to another woman

long after death
in a different world

1983

In the Wake of Home

1.

You sleep in a room with bluegreen curtains
posters   a pile of animals on the bed
A woman and a man who love you
and each other   slip the door ajar
you are almost asleep   they crouch in turn
to stroke your hair   you never wake

This happens every night for years.
This never happened.

2.

Your lips   steady   never say
It should have been this way
That's not what you say
You   so carefully not asking, *Why?*
Your eyes   looking straight in mine
remind me of a woman's
auburn hair   my mother's hair
but you never saw that hair

The family coil   so twisted, tight and loose
anyone trying to leave
has to strafe the field
burn the premises down

3.

The home houses
mirages   memory fogs the kitchen panes
the rush-hour traffic outside
has the same old ebb and flow
Out on the darkening block

somebody calls you home
night after night   then never again
Useless for you to know
they tried to do what they could
before they left for good

4.
The voice that used to call you home
has gone off on the wind
beaten into thinnest air
whirling down other streets
or maybe the mouth was burnt to ash
maybe the tongue was torn out
brownlung has stolen the breath
or fear has stolen the breath
maybe under another name
it sings on AM radio:
And if you knew, what would you know?

5.
But you will be drawn to places
where generations lie
side by side with each other:
fathers, mothers and children
in the family prayerbook
or the country burying-ground
You will hack your way through the bush
to the Jodensavanne
where the gravestones are black with mould
You will stare at old family albums
with their smiles   their resemblances
You will want to believe that nobody
wandered off   became strange
no woman dropped her baby and ran
no father took off for the hills

no axe splintered the door
—that once at least it was all in order
and nobody came to grief

6.
Anytime you go back
where absence began
the kitchen faucet sticks in a way you know
you have to pull the basement door
in before drawing the bolt
the last porch-step is still loose
the water from the tap
is the old drink of water
Any time you go back
the familiar underpulse
will start its throbbing: *Home, home!*
and the hole torn and patched over
will gape unseen again

7.
Even where love has run thin
the child's soul musters strength
calling on dust-motes   song on the radio
closet-floor of galoshes
stray cat   piles of autumn leaves
whatever comes along
—the rush of purpose to make a life
worth living past abandonment
building the layers up again
over the torn hole   filling in

8.
And what of the stern and faithful aunt
the fierce grandmother   the anxious sister
the good teacher   the one

who stood at the crossing when you had to cross
the woman hired to love you
the skeleton who held out a crust
the breaker of rules   the one
who is neither a man nor a woman   the one
who warmed the liquid vein of life
and day after day whatever the need
handed it on to you?
You who did and had to do
so much for yourself   this was done for you
by someone who did what they could
when others left for good

9.
You imagine an alley   a little kingdom
where the mother-tongue is spoken
a village of shelters   woven
or sewn of hides   in a long-ago way
a shanty standing up
at the edge of sharecropped fields
a tenement where life is seized by the teeth
a farm battened down on snowswept plains
a porch with rubber-plant and glider
on a steep city street
You imagine the people would all be there
fathers mothers and children
the ones you were promised would all be there
eating   arguing   working
trying to get on with life
you imagine this used to be
for everyone   everywhere

10.
What if I told you your home
is this continent of the homeless

of children sold   taken by force
driven from their mothers' land
killed by their mothers to save from capture
—this continent of changed names and mixed-up blood
of languages tabooed
diasporas unrecorded
undocumented refugees
underground railroads   trails of tears
What if I tell you your home
is this planet of warworn children
women and children standing in line or milling
endlessly calling each others' names
What if I tell you, you are not different
it's the family albums that lie
—will any of this comfort you
and how should this comfort you?

11.
The child's soul carries on
in the wake of home
building a complicated house
a tree-house without a tree
finding places for everything
the song   the stray cat   the skeleton
The child's soul musters strength
where the holes were torn
but there are no miracles:
even children become exhausted
And how shall they comfort each other
who have come young to grief?
Who will number the grains of loss
and what would comfort be?

1983

What Was, Is;
What Might Have Been, Might Be

What's kept.   What's lost.   A snap decision.
Burn the archives.   Let them rot.
Begin by going ten years back.

A woman walks downstairs in a brownstone
in Brooklyn.   Late that night, some other night
snow crystals swarm in her hair
at the place we say, So long.

I've lost something.   I'm not sure what it is.
I'm going through my files.

Jewel-weed flashing
blue fire against an iron fence
Her head bent to a mailbox
long fingers ringed in gold   in red-eyed
golden serpents

the autumn sun
burns like a beak off the cars
parked along Riverside   we so deep in talk
in burnt September grass

I'm trying for exactitude
in the files I handle worn and faded labels
And how she drove, and danced, and fought, and worked
and loved, and sang, and hated
dashed into the record store   then out
with the Stevie Wonder   back in the car
flew on

Worn and faded labels . . . This was
our glamor for each other
underlined in bravado

Could it have been another way:
could we have been respectful comrades
parallel warriors   none of that
fast-falling

could we have kept a clean
and decent slate

1984

For an Occupant

Did the fox speak to you?
Did the small brush-fires on the hillside
smoke her out?
Were you standing on the porch
not the kitchen porch   the front
one of poured concrete   full in the rising moon
and did she appear   wholly on her own
asking no quarter   wandering by
on impulse   up the drive   and on
into the pine-woods
but were you standing there
at the moment of moon and burnished light
leading your own life   till she caught your eye
asking no charity
but did she speak to you?

1983

Emily Carr

I try to conjure the kind of joy
you tracked through the wildwoods where the tribes
had set up their poles   what brought you
how by boat, water, wind, you found
yourself facing the one great art
of your native land, your life

All I know is, it is here
even postcard-size can't diminish
the great eye, nostril, tongue
the wave of the green hills
the darkblue crest of sky   the white
and yellow fog bundled behind the green

You were alone in this
Nobody knew or cared
how to paint the way you saw
or what you saw   Alone
you walked up to the sacred and disregarded
with your canvas, your box of colors

saying *Wait for me* and the crumbling
totem poles held still
while you sat down on your stool, your knees
spread wide, and let the mist
roll in past your shoulders
bead your rough shawl, your lashes

Wait for me, I have waited so long for you
But you never said that   I

am ashamed to have thought it
You had no personal leanings
You brushed in the final storm-blue stroke
and gave it its name: *Skidegate Pole*

1984

Poetry: I

Someone at a table under a brown metal lamp
is studying the history of poetry.
Someone in the library at closing-time
has learned to say *modernism,*
trope, vatic, text.
She is listening for shreds of music.
He is searching for his name
back in the old country.
They cannot learn without teachers.
They are like us   what we were
if you remember.

In a corner of night a voice
is crying in a kind of whisper:
More!

Can you remember?   when we thought
the poets taught   how to live?
That is not the voice of a critic
nor a common reader
it is someone young   in anger
hardly knowing what to ask
who finds our lines   our glosses
wanting   in this world.

1985

Poetry: II, Chicago

Whatever a poet is
at the point of conception   is
conceived in these projects
of beige and grey bricks   Yes, poets are born
in wasted tracts like these   whatever color, sex
comes to term in this winter's driving nights
And the child pushes like a spear
a cry   through cracked cement   through zero air
a spear, a cry of green   Yes, poets endure
these schools of fear   balked yet unbroken
where so much gets broken: trust
windows   pride   the mothertongue

Wherever a poet is born   enduring
depends on the frailest of chances:
Who listened to your murmuring
over your little rubbish   who let you be
who gave you the books
who let you know you were not
alone   showed you the the twist
of old strands   raffia, hemp or silk
the beaded threads   the fiery lines
saying: *This belongs to you   you have the right*
you belong to the song
of your mothers and fathers   You have a people

1984

Poetry: III

Even if we knew the children were all asleep
and healthy   the ledgers balanced   the water running
clear in the pipes
                    and all the prisoners free

Even if every word we wrote by then
were honest   the sheer heft
of our living behind it
                        not these sometimes
lax, indolent lines
                    these litanies

Even if we were told   not just by friends
that this was honest work

Even if each of us didn't wear
a brass locket with a picture
of a strangled woman   a girlchild sewn through the crotch

Even if someone had told us, young: *This is not a key*
nor a peacock feather
                        not a kite nor a telephone
This is the kitchen sink   the grinding-stone

would we give ourselves
more calmly over   feel less criminal joy
when the thing comes   as it does come
clarifying grammar
and the fixed and mutable stars—?

1984

Baltimore: a fragment from the Thirties

Medical textbooks propped in a dusty window.
Outside, it's summer.   Heat
swamping stretched awnings, battering dark-green shades.
The Depression, Monument Street,
ice-wagons trailing melt, the Hospital
with its segregated morgues . . .
I'm five years old and trying to be perfect
walking hand-in-hand with my father.
A Black man halts beside us
croaks in a terrible voice, *I'm hungry* . . .
I'm a lucky child but I've read about beggars—
how the good give, the evil turn away.
But I want to turn away.   My father gives.
We walk in silence.   Why did he sound like that?
Is it evil to be frightened?   I want to ask.
He has no roof in his mouth,

> my father says at last.

1985

New York

For B. and C.

        at your table
telephone rings
              every four minutes
                       talk
of terrible things
            the papers bringing
no good news
           and burying the worst

Cut-up fruit in cutglass bowls
good for you
            French Market coffee
cut with hot milk
            crying together
wanting to save this
            how we are when we meet
all our banners out
            do we deceive each other
do we speak of the dead we sit with
do we mourn in secret
            do we taste the sweetness
of life in the center of pain

I wanted to say to you
until the revolution this is happiness
yet was afraid to praise
            even with such skeptic turn
of phrase   so shrugged a smile

1985

Homage to Winter

You: a woman too old
for passive contemplation
caught staring out a window
at bird-of-paradise spikes
jewelled with rain, across an alley
It's winter in this land
of roses, roses   sometimes
the fog lies thicker around you than your past
sometimes the Pacific radiance
scours the air to lapis
In this new world you feel
backward along the hem of your whole life
questioning every breadth
Nights you can watch the moon shed skin after skin
over and over, always a shape
of imbalance except
at birth and in the full
You, still trying to learn
how to live, what must be done
though in death you will be complete
whatever you do
But death is not the answer.

On these flat green leaves
light skates like a golden blade
high in the dull-green pine
sit two mushroom-colored doves
afterglow overflows
across the bungalow roof
between the signs for the three-way stop
over everything that is:
the cotton pants stirring on the line, the

empty Coke can by the fence
onto the still unflowering
mysterious acacia
and a sudden chill takes the air

Backward you dream to a porch
you stood on a year ago
snow flying quick as thought
sticking to your shoulder   gone
Blue shadows, ridged and fading
on a snow-swept road
the shortest day of the year
Backward you dream to glare ice
and ice-wet pussywillows
to Riverside Drive, the wind
cut loose from Hudson's Bay
driving tatters into your face
And back you come at last to that room
without a view, where webs of frost
blinded the panes at noon
where already you had begun
to make the visible world your conscience
asking things: *What can you tell me?*
what am I doing?   what must I do?

1985

Blue Rock

For Myriam Díaz-Diocaretz

Your chunk of lapis-lazuli shoots its stain
blue into the wineglass on the table

the full moon moving up the sky is plain
as the dead rose and the live buds on one stem

No, this isn't Persian poetry I'm quoting:
all this is here in North America

where I sit trying to kindle fire
from what's already on fire:

the light of a blue rock from Chile swimming
in the apricot liquid called "eye of the swan".

This is a chunk of your world, a piece of its heart:
split from the rest, does it suffer?

You needn't tell me.   Sometimes I hear it singing
by the waters of Babylon, in a strange land

sometimes it just lies heavy in my hand
with the heaviness of silent seismic knowledge

a blue rock in a foreign land, an exile
excised but never separated

from the gashed heart, its mountains,
winter rains, language, native sorrow.

At the end of the twentieth century
cardiac graphs of torture reply to poetry

line by line: in North America
the strokes of the stylus continue

the figures of terror are reinvented
all night, after I turn the lamp off, blotting

wineglass, rock and roses, leaving pages
like this scrawled with mistakes and love,

falling asleep; but the stylus does not sleep,
cruelly the drum revolves, cruelty writes its name.

Once when I wrote poems they did not change
left overnight on the page

they stayed as they were and daylight broke
on the lines, as on the clotheslines in the yard

heavy with clothes forgotten or left out
for a better sun next day

But now I know what happens while I sleep
and when I wake the poem has changed:

the facts have dilated it, or cancelled it;
and in every morning's light, your rock is there.

1985

Yom Kippur 1984

I drew solitude over me, on the lone shore.
—Robinson Jeffers, "Prelude"

For whoever does not afflict his soul throughout
this day, shall be cut off from his people.
—Leviticus 23:29

What is a Jew in solitude?
What would it mean not to feel lonely or afraid
far from your own or those you have called your own?
What is a woman in solitude: a queer woman or man?
In the empty street, on the empty beach, in the desert
what in this world as it is can solitude mean?

The glassy, concrete octagon suspended from the cliffs
with its electric gate, its perfected privacy
is not what I mean
the pick-up with a gun parked at a turn-out in Utah or the Golan
            Heights
is not what I mean
the poet's tower facing the western ocean, acres of forest planted to
            the east, the woman reading in the cabin, her
            attack dog suddenly risen
is not what I mean

Three thousand miles from what I once called home
I open a book searching for some lines I remember
about flowers, something to bind me to this coast as lilacs in the
            dooryard once
bound me back there—yes, lupines on a burnt mountainside,
something that bloomed and faded and was written down
in the poet's book, forever:
Opening the poet's book
I find the hatred in the poet's heart: . . . *the hateful-eyed*

75

and human-bodied are all about me: you that love multitude may have
them

Robinson Jeffers, multitude
is the blur flung by distinct forms against these landward valleys
and the farms that run down to the sea; the lupines
are multitude, and the torched poppies, the grey Pacific unrolling
its scrolls of surf,
and the separate persons, stooped
over sewing machines in denim dust, bent under the shattering
skies of harvest
who sleep by shifts in never-empty beds have their various dreams
Hands that pick, pack, steam, stitch, strip, stuff, shell, scrape,
scour, belong to a brain like no other
Must I argue the love of multitude in the blur or defend
a solitude of barbed-wire and searchlights, the survivalist's final
solution, have I a choice?

To wander far from your own or those you have called your own
to hear strangeness calling you from far away
and walk in that direction, long and far, not calculating risk
to go to meet the Stranger without fear or weapon, protection
nowhere on your mind
(the Jew on the icy, rutted road on Christmas Eve prays for another
Jew
the woman in the ungainly twisting shadows of the street: *Make*
those be a woman's footsteps; as if she could believe in a
woman's god)

Find someone like yourself.   Find others.
Agree you will never desert each other.
Understand that any rift among you
means power to those who want to do you in.
Close to the center, safety; toward the edges, danger.
But I have a nightmare to tell: I am trying to say

that to be with my people is my dearest wish
but that I also love strangers
that I crave separateness
I hear myself stuttering these words
to my worst friends and my best enemies
who watch for my mistakes in grammar
my mistakes in love.
This is the day of atonement; but do my people forgive me?
If a cloud knew loneliness and fear, I would be that cloud.

To love the Stranger, to love solitude—am I writing merely about
          privilege
about drifting from the center, drawn to edges,
a privilege we can't afford in the world that is,
who are hated as being of our kind: faggot kicked into the icy
          river, woman dragged from her stalled car
into the mist-struck mountains, used and hacked to death
young scholar shot at the university gates on a summer evening
          walk, his prizes and studies nothing, nothing
          availing his Blackness
Jew deluded that she's escaped the tribe, the laws of her exclusion,
          the men too holy to touch her hand;   Jew who has
          turned her back
on *midrash* and *mitzvah* (yet wears the *chai* on a thong between her
          breasts) hiking alone
found with a swastika carved in her back at the foot of the cliffs
          (did she die as queer or as Jew?)

Solitude, O taboo, endangered species
on the mist-struck spur of the mountain, I want a gun to defend
          you
In the desert, on the deserted street, I want what I can't have:
your elder sister, Justice, her great peasant's hand outspread
her eye, half-hooded, sharp and true
And I ask myself, have I thrown courage away?

have I traded off something I don't name?
To what extreme will I go to meet the extremist?
What will I do to defend my want or anyone's want to search for
            her spirit-vision
far from the protection of those she has called her own?
Will I find O solitude
your plumes, your breasts, your hair
against my face, as in childhood, your voice like the mockingbird's
singing *Yes, you are loved, why else this song?*
in the old places, anywhere?

What is a Jew in solitude?
What is a woman in solitude, a queer woman or man?
When the winter flood-tides wrench the tower from the rock,
            crumble the prophet's headland, and the farms slide
            into the sea
when leviathan is endangered and Jonah becomes revenger
when center and edges are crushed together, the extremities
            crushed together on which the world was founded
when our souls crash together, Arab and Jew, howling our
            loneliness within the tribes
when the refugee child and the exile's child re-open the blasted and
            forbidden city
when we who refuse to be women and men as women and men are
            chartered, tell our stories of solitude spent in
            multitude
in that world as it may be, newborn and haunted, what will
            solitude mean?

1984–1985

Edges

In the sleepless sleep of dawn, in the dreamless dream
the kingfisher cuts through   flashing
spirit-fire from his wings   bluer than violet's edge
the slice of those wings

5 a.m., first light, hoboes of the past
are leaning through the window, what freightcars
did they hop here   I thought I'd left behind?
Their hands are stretched out but not for bread
they are past charity, they want me to hear   their names

Outside in the world where so much is possible
sunrise rekindles and the kingfisher—
the living kingfisher, not that flash of vision—
darts where the creek drags her wetness over stump and stone
where poison oak reddens   acacia pods collect
curled and secretive against the bulkhead

and the firstlight ghosts go transparent
while the homeless line for bread

1985

III

Contradictions:
Tracking Poems

1.

Look: this is January   the worst onslaught
is ahead of us   Don't be lured
by these soft grey afternoons   these sunsets cut
from pink and violet tissue-paper   by the thought
the days are lengthening
Don't let the solstice fool you:
our lives will always be
a stew of contradictions
the worst moment of winter can come in April
when the peepers are stubbornly still   and our bodies
plod on without conviction
and our thoughts cramp down before the sheer
arsenal of everything that tries us:
this battering, blunt-edged life

2.

Heart of cold.   Bones of cold.   Scalp of cold.
the grey   the black   the blond   the red
hairs on a skull of cold.   Within that skull
the thought of war   the sovereign thought
the coldest of all thought.   Dreaming shut down
everything kneeling down to cold   intelligence
smirking with cold   memory
squashed and frozen cold   breath
half held-in for cold.   The freezing people
of a freezing nation   eating
luxury food or garbage
frozen tongues licking the luxury meat
or the pizza-crust   the frozen eyes
welded to other eyes   also frozen
the cold hands trying to stroke   the coldest sex.
Heart of cold   Sex of cold   Intelligence of cold
My country   wedged fast in history
stuck in the ice

3.

My mouth hovers across your breasts
in the short grey winter afternoon
in this bed   we are delicate
and tough   so hot with joy we amaze ourselves
tough   and delicate   we play rings
around each other   our daytime candle burns
with its peculiar light   and if the snow
begins to fall outside   filling the branches
and if the night falls   without announcement
these are the pleasures of winter
sudden, wild and delicate   your fingers
exact   my tongue exact at the same moment
stopping to laugh at a joke
my love   hot on your scent   on the cusp of winter

4.

He slammed his hand across my face   and I
let him do that until   I stopped letting him do it
so I'm in for life.

. . . . he kept saying I was crazy, he'd lock me up
until I went to Women's Lib and they
told me he'd been abusing me as much
as if he'd hit me: emotional abuse.
They told me how to answer back.   That I could
answer back.   But my brother-in-law's a shrink
with the State.   I have to watch my step.
If I stay just within bounds they can't come and get me.
Women's Lib taught me the words to say
to remind myself and him I'm a person with rights
like anyone.   But answering back's no answer.

5.

She is carrying my madness   and I dread her
avoid her when I can
She walks along I.S. 93   howling
in her bare feet
She is number 6375411
in a cellblock in Arkansas
and I dread what she is paying for   that is mine
She has fallen asleep at last in the battered
women's safe-house   and I dread
her dreams   that I also dream
If never I become exposed or confined like this
what am I hiding
O sister of nausea   of broken ribs   of isolation
what is this freedom I protect   how is it mine

6.

Dear Adrienne:
                    I'm calling you up tonight
as I might call up a friend   as I might call up a ghost
to ask what you intend to do
with the rest of your life.   Sometimes you act
as if you have all the time there is.
I worry about you when I see this.
The prime of life, old age
aren't what they used to be;
making a good death isn't either,
now you can walk around the corner of a wall
and see a light
that already has blown your past away.
Somewhere in Boston   beautiful literature
is being read around the clock
by writers   to signify
their dislike of this.
I hope you've got something in mind.
I hope you have some idea
about the rest of your life.
                              In sisterhood,

                                        Adrienne

7.

Dear Adrienne,
                    I feel signified by pain
from my breastbone through my left shoulder down
through my elbow into my wrist is a thread of pain
I am typing this instead of writing by hand
because my wrist on the right side
blooms and rushes with pain
like a neon bulb
You ask me how I'm going to live
the rest of my life
Well, nothing is predictable with pain
Did the old poets write of this?
—in its odd spaces, free,
many have sung and battled—
But I'm already living the rest of my life
not under conditions of my choosing
wired   into pain
                    rider on the slow train

                                        Yours, Adrienne

8.

I'm afraid of prison.   Have been all these years.
Afraid they'll take my aspirin away
and of other things as well:
beatings   damp and cold   I have my fears.
Unable one day to get up and walk
to do what must be done
Prison as idea   it fills me
with fear   this exposure to my own weakness
at someone else's whim
I watched that woman go over the barbed-wire fence
at the peace encampment
                                        the wheelchair rider
I didn't want to do what she did
I thought, They'll get her for this
I thought, We are not such victims.

9.

Tearing but not yet torn: this page
The long late-winter rage
wild rain on the windshield
clenched stems   unyielding sticks
of maple, birch   bleached grass   the range
of things resisting change
And this is how I am
and this is how you are
when we resist the charmer's open sesame
the thief's light-fingered touch
staying closed because we will
not give ourselves away
until the agent   the manipulator   the false toucher
has left   and it is May

10.

Night   over the great and the little worlds
of Brooklyn   the shredded communities
in Chicago   Argentina   Poland
in Holyoke Massachusetts   Amsterdam   Manchester
   England
Night falls   the day of atonement begins
in how many divided hearts   how many defiant lives
Toronto   Managua   St. Johnsbury
and the great and little worlds of the women
Something ancient passes across the earth
lifting the dust of the blasted ghettos
You ask if I will eat and I say, Yes,
I have never fasted
but something crosses my life
not a shadow   the reflection of a fire

11.

I came out of the hospital like a woman
who'd watched a massacre
not knowing how to tell
my adhesions   the lingering infections
from the pain on the streets
In my room on Yom Kippur they took me off morphine
I saw shadows on the wall   the dying and the dead
They said Christian Phalangists did it
then Kol Nidre on the radio   and my own
unhoused spirit   trying to find a home
Was it then or another day
in what order did it happen
I thought   *They call this elective surgery*
but we all have died of this.

12.

Violence as purification: the one idea.
One massacre great enough to undo another
one last-ditch operation to solve the problem
of the old operation that was bungled
Look: I have lain on their tables under their tools
under their drugs   from the center of my body
a voice bursts   against these methods
(wherever you made a mistake
batter with radiation   defoliate   cut away)
and yes, there are merciful debridements
but burns turn into rotting flesh
for reasons of vengeance and neglect.
I have been too close to septic too many times
to play with either violence or non-violence.

13.

Trapped in one idea, you can't have your feelings,
feelings are always about more than one thing.
You drag yourself back home and it is autumn
you can't concentrate, you can't lie on the couch
so you drive yourself for hours on the quiet roads
crying at the wheel   watching the colors
deepening, fading   and winter is coming
and you long for one idea
one simple, huge idea to take this weight
and you know you will never find it, never
because you don't want to find it
You will drive and cry and come home and eat
and listen to the news
and slowly even at winter's edge
the feelings come back in their shapes
and colors   conflicting   they come back
   they are changed

14.

Lately in my dreams I hear long sentences
meaningless in ordinary American
like, *Your mother, too, was a missionary of poets*
and in another dream one of my old teachers
shows me a letter of reference
he has written for me, in a language
I know to be English but cannot understand,
telling me it's in "transformational grammar"
and that the student who typed the letter
does not understand this grammar either.
Lately I dreamed about my father,
how I found him, alive, seated on an old chair.
I think what he said to me was,
You don't know how lonely I am.

15.

You who think I find words for everything,
and you for whom I write this,
how can I show you what I'm barely
coming into possession of, invisible luggage
of more than fifty years, looking at first
glance like everyone else's, turning up
at the airport carousel
and the waiting for it, knowing what nobody
would steal must eventually come round—
feeling obsessed, peculiar, longing?

16.

It's true, these last few years I've lived
watching myself in the act of loss—the art of losing,
Elizabeth Bishop called it, but for me no art
only badly-done exercises
acts of the heart forced to question
its presumptions in this world   its mere excitements
acts of the body forced to measure
all instincts against pain
acts of parting   trying to let go
without giving up   yes   Elizabeth   a city here
a village there   a sister, comrade, cat
and more   no art to this but anger

17.

I have backroads I take   to places
like the hospital where night pain
is never tended enough but I can drive
under the overlacing boughs
of wineglass elm, oak, maple
from Mosquitoville to Wells River
along the double track with the greened hump
the slope with the great sugar-grove
New Age talk calls it "visualizing"   but I know
under torture I would travel
from the West Barnet burying-ground
to Joe's Brook   by heart   I know
all of those roads by heart
by heart I know what, and all, I have left behind

18.

The problem, unstated till now, is how
to live in a damaged body
in a world where pain is meant to be gagged
uncured   un-grieved-over   The problem is
to connect, without hysteria, the pain
of any one's body with the pain of the body's world
For it is the body's world
they are trying to destroy forever
The best world is the body's world
filled with creatures   filled with dread
misshapen so   yet the best we have
our raft among the abstract worlds
and how I longed to live on this earth
walking her boundaries   never counting the cost

19.

If to feel is to be unreliable
don't listen to us
if to be in pain is to be predictable
embittered   bullying
then don't listen to us
If we're in danger of mistaking
our personal trouble for the pain on the streets
don't listen to us
if my fury at being grounded frightens you
take off on your racing skis
in your beautiful tinted masks
Trapped in one idea, you can't have feelings
Without feelings perhaps you can feel like a god

20.

The tobacco fields lie fallow   the migrant pickers
no longer visible
where undocumented intelligences travailed
on earth they had no stake in
though the dark leaves growing beneath white veils
were beautiful   and the barns opened out like fans
All this of course could have been done differently
This valley itself: one more contradiction
the paradise fields   the brute skyscrapers
the pesticidal wells

I have been wanting for years
to write a poem   equal to these
material forces
and I have always failed
I wasn't looking for a muse
only a reader by whom   I could not be mistaken

21.

The cat-tails blaze in the corner   sunflowers
shed their pale fiery dust   on the dark stove-lid
others stand guard   heads bowed   over the garden
the fierce and flaring garden you have made
out of your woes and expectations
tilled into the earth   I circle close to your mind
crash into it sometimes   as you crash into mine
Given this strip of earth   given mere love
should we not be happy?
but happiness comes and goes as it comes and goes
the safe-house is temporary   the garden
lies open to vandals
this whole valley is one more contradiction
and more will be asked of us   we will ask more

22.

In a bald skull sits our friend   in a helmet
of third-degree burns
her quizzical melancholy grace
her irreplaceable self   in utter peril
In the radioactive desert walks a woman
in a black dress   white-haired   steady
as the luminous hand of a clock
in circles she walks   knitting
and unknitting her scabbed fingers
Her face is expressionless   shall we pray to her
shall we speak of the loose pine-needles   how they shook
like the pith of country summers
from the sacks of pitchblende ore in the tin-roofed shack
where it all began
Shall we accuse her of denial
first of the self   then of the mixed virtue
of the purest science   shall we be wise for her
in hindsight   shall we scream *It has come to this*
Shall we praise her   shall we let her wander
the atomic desert   in peace?

23.

You know the Government must have pushed them to settle,
the chemical industries   and pay
that hush-money to the men
who landed out there at twenty   not for belief
but because of who they were   and were called psychos
when they said their bodies contained dioxin
like memories they didn't want to keep
whose kids came out deformed
You know nothing has changed   no respect or grief
for the losers of a lost war everyone hated
nobody sent them to school like heroes
if they started sueing for everything that was done
there would be no end   there would be a beginning
My country   wedged fast in history
stuck in the ice

24.

Someone said to me: *It's just that we don't*
know how to cope with the loss of memory.
When your own grandfather doesn't know you
when your mother thinks you're somebody else
it's a terrible thing.
Now just like that is this idea
that the universe will forget us, everything we've done
will go nowhere
no one will know who we were.
No one will know who we were!

Not the young who will never   Nor even the old folk
who knew us when we were young   insatiable
for recognition from them
trying so fiercely not to be them
counting on them to know us   anywhere

25.

Did anyone ever know who we were
if *we* means more than a handful?
flower of a generation   young white men
cut off in the named, commemorated wars
I stare   Jewish   into that loss
for which all names become unspeakable
not ever just the best and brightest
but the most wretched and bedevilled
the obscure   the strange   the driven
the twins   the dwarfs   the geniuses   the gay
But ours was not the only loss
(to whom does annihilation speak
as if for the first time?)

26.

You: air-driven   reft   from the tuber-bitten soil
that was your portion   from the torched-out village
the Marxist study-group   the Zionist cell
café or *cheder*   Zaddik or Freudian   straight or gay
woman or man   O you
stripped   bared   appalled
stretched to mere spirit   yet still physical
your irreplaceable knowledge   lost
at the mud-slick bottom of the world
how you held fast   with your bone-meal fingers
to yourselves   each other   and strangers
how you touched   held-up from falling
what was already half-cadaver
how your life-cry taunted extinction
with its wild, crude   *so what?*
Grief for you has rebellion at its heart
it cannot simply mourn
You: air-driven: reft: are yet our teachers
trying to speak to us in sleep
trying to help us wake

27.

The Tolstoyans   the Afro-American slaves
knew this: you could be killed
for teaching people to read and write
I used to think the worst affliction
was to be forbidden pencil and paper
well, Ding Ling recited poems to prison walls
for years of the Cultural Revolution
and truly, the magic of written characters
looms and dwindles   shrinks small   grows swollen
depending on where you stand
and what is in your hand
and who can read and why
I think now the worst affliction
is not to know who you are or have been
I have learned this in part
from writers   Reading and writing
aren't sacred   yet people have been killed
as if they were

28.

This high summer we love will pour its light
the fields grown rich and ragged in one strong moment
then before we're ready will crash into autumn
with a violence we can't accept
a bounty we can't forgive
Night frost will strike when the noons are warm
the pumpkins wildly glowing   the green tomatoes
straining huge on the vines
queen anne and blackeyed susan will straggle rusty
as the milkweed stakes her claim
she who will stand at last   dark sticks barely rising
up through the snow   her testament of continuation
We'll dream of a longer summer
but this is the one we have:
I lay my sunburnt hand
on your table: this is the time we have

29.

You who think I find words for everything
this is enough for now
cut it short   cut loose from my words

You for whom I write this
in the night hours when the wrecked cartilage
sifts round the mystical jointure of the bones
when the insect of detritus crawls
from shoulder to elbow to wristbone
remember: the body's pain and the pain on the streets
are not the same   but you can learn
from the edges that blur   O you who love clear edges
more than anything   watch the edges that blur

1983–1985

Notes

"Sources": The phrase "an end to suffering" was evoked by a sentence in Nadine Gordimer's *Burger's Daughter:* "No one knows where the end of suffering will begin."

"North American Time: IX": Julia de Burgos (1914–1953), Puerto Rican poet and revolutionary who died on the streets of New York City.

"Dreams Before Waking": "Hasta tu país cambió. Lo has cambiado tú mismo" ("Even your country has changed. You yourself have changed it"). These lines, from Morejón's "Elogio de la Dialéctica," and Georgina Herrera's poem "Como Presentación, Como Disculpa" can be found in Margaret Randall, ed., *Breaking the Silences: Twentieth Century Poetry by Cuban Women* (1982). Pulp Press, 3868 MPO, Vancouver, Canada V6B 3Z3.

"One Kind of Terror: A Love Poem: 6": "Now you have touched the women, you have struck a rock, you have dislodged a boulder, you will be crushed." Freedom song sung by African women in mass demonstration in Pretoria, 1956, in which 20,000 women gathered to protest the issue of passes to women. See Hilda Bernstein, *For Their Triumphs and for Their Tears,* International Defence and Aid Fund for Southern Africa, 1975.

"In the Wake of Home: 5": The Jodensavanne is an abandoned Jewish settlement in Surinam whose ruins exist in a jungle on the Cassipoera River.

"Emily Carr": Canadian painter (1871–1945). At the height of her powers she painted, with deep respect, the disappearing totem poles of the Northwest Coast Indians. See Doris Shadbolt, *The Art of Emily Carr* (Seattle: University of Washington Press, 1979).

"Yom Kippur 1984": The epigraph and quoted lines from Robinson Jeffers come from *The Women at Point Sur and Other Poems* (New York: Liveright, 1977).

"Contradictions: 16": See Elizabeth Bishop, *The Complete Poems 1927–1979* (New York: Farrar, Straus & Giroux, 1983), p. 173.

"Contradictions: 26": See Cynthia Ozick, *Art and Ardor* (New York: Farrar, Straus & Giroux, 1984), p. 255: "the glorious So What: the life-cry."

"Contradictions: 27": Ding Ling, leading Chinese novelist and major literary figure in the Revolutionary government under Mao. Exiled in 1957 for writing too critically and independently. Imprisoned as a counterrevolutionary in 1970; cleared of all charges in 1976 at the end of the Cultural Revolution.